Comp

Primary Prayers

Complete Primary Prayers

Helping
your school
talk with
God

TONY BOWER

kevin
mayhew

First published in 2007 by

KEVIN MAYHEW LTD
Buxhall, Stowmarket, Suffolk, IP14 3BW
E-mail: info@kevinmayhewltd.com
www.kevinmayhew.com

9 8 7 6 5 4 3 2 1 0
ISBN 978 1 84417 828 5
Catalogue No. 1501042

Cover design by Sara-Jane Came
Typesetting by Richard Weaver

Printed and bound in Great Britain

Contents

*Special thanks to Claire Bower and Debbie Green
for helping to edit, type and collate
this book of prayers*

Introduction

These primary school prayers can be used in assembly or class. They are written to enable children to build relationships with God by talking to him and with him about the things that concern them:

- creation and the world
- themselves
- situations they face
- other people
- school life

At the beginning of the book there's a special section with ideas to inspire children to pray their own prayers as groups and as individuals.

Encourage the children to end each prayer with 'in Jesus' name we pray, amen,' or just a simple 'amen'.

There's also an opportunity to raise pupils' awareness of the Bible by using the sections based on selected Psalms and other parts of Scripture.

Creative ways to pray

It's good to encourage children to contribute to prayers in school. Children usually have no problem speaking openly with Jesus, but each has their own 'comfort zone' which needs to be explored sensitively.

For example, some might want to think carefully about their prayers, writing them out during class time to be read aloud later, either in an assembly or at going-home time. Others might be ready to open up right away.

To broaden your children's experiences of speaking with God here are some suggestions which have all proved successful in encouraging both groups – those who already feel at ease praying aloud and those who might be hesitant.

Alphabet prayer

Think of things to thank God for and compose an A-Z prayer of all the various items on your list. This could go on the classroom wall. Alternatively, this could be undertaken as a group/class or individual exercise.

Object prayer

Take something visual to class that will be a prompt and an aid to prayer. For example, a family photo to think about and pray for our families; a picture of creation to think of the world; a musical instrument to give praises for music; the list of objects to stimulate prayer are numerous but too many to list here.

Picture prayer

A similar idea to the one before, but this time solely focused on the use of pictures or photographs.

Light prayer

Light is a very popular and powerful symbol. A lit candle is often used in schools during assembly time. Advent candles are also very popular in churches. Suggest some class prayers thinking about light and what it means to us. You could also make connections to Jesus, saying that he is the light of the world.

'Describing' prayers

You could do this as a collective class prayer, or in groups or individually. Give each child an opportunity to sum up God in one word. You could prepare them by selecting some readings from the Bible to help them think.

News prayers

Take in newspapers and talk to the children about some of the stories covered. Then suggest that they pray for the world. The format of this session and the type of stories you select will depend on the age of the class and the appropriateness of the coverage.

Sensory prayers

Use objects that have a different effect on our senses. Find a range of objects for the children to touch (you could even turn this into a fun exercise by blindfolding the children and seeing if they can guess what they are touching). Move on to different things to smell, different objects or instruments that make a variety of sounds. Use the exercise to reflect on our senses and the way the human body is made (a nice link with science and RE). Give thanks for our senses and the way in which we were created.

Creation prayers

Take the class outside and ask them to take a good look at what's around them – then suggest that they close their eyes and listen quietly. Then ask the group to give thankful prayers for the things they have seen and heard.

This works well in just about any weather condition apart from when it's tipping down with rain, blowing a gale, freezing and anything else which would cause you to dash inside for the warmth and comfort of the classroom radiator!

World prayers

Use a map or globe of the world as a visual aid as you talk about some of the different countries and cultures in the world. Invite prayers for the different places and different races. You could also focus on the fact that we are very different from one another and discuss the diversity of the population.

Invite pupils from other countries to share information about their country and culture by establishing weblinks or using existing ones.

Creation and our world

Our world

Our world
is BIG
and round,
so the scientists
have found.
It's filled with
land, sea and air,
all kinds of animals
who share
our planet,
our earth,
our world,
with us.
The great BIG
family of God's creativity.

Life-giving God,
The universe we live in you
  created.
The planet we play upon you
  created.
The stars in space you
  created.
The hot, burning sun you
  created.
The bright, shining moon you
  created.
The person that I am you
  created.

Colours

Father God,
Thank you
that the world
is full of wonderful colours
and not just made
in black and white.
Thank you
that you made people
to be colourful too:
black
white
brown
yellow
red
faces;
blue
brown
green
grey
eyes;
black
brown
ginger
blond
hair.
So many different colours
for us to see
and enjoy.

Rainy day

Dear Creator God,
Thank you
for the rain
that makes the flowers grow,
that helps the rivers flow,
that helps the harvest grow,
that helps the world we know
to flow with LIFE!

Air!

Life-giving God,
Thank you
for the air we breathe.
We cannot see it
but we know
we cannot live without it.
Thank you that
we have been given
the breath of life
through you.
And although we cannot see
you,
we cannot live
without you.

Sunny day

Creator God,
Thank you
for the sun that helps the
flowers grow,
that makes our faces glow,
that helps the harvest grow,
that makes the world we know
to glow with LIFE.

Animal prayer

Creator God,
Thank you for all the animals
that live in our world.
Thank you for the lions and
their super claws.
Thank you for the pandas
and their big, black eyes.
Thank you for the polar bears
and their furry, white coats.
Thank you for the seals
and their slippery skin.
Thank you for the penguins
and their waddling walk.
Thank you for the crocodiles
and their snapping jaws.
Thank you for the orang-
utans and their swinging
arms.
Thank you for all the animals
that live in our world.

Sand

Father God,
Thank you
for the sand
that gets between my toes,
that goes up my nose,
sticks on my face,
and gets all over the place.
Thank you, that sand
is good fun to play with,
make sandcastles with
and all kinds of creative
creations.
Thank you,
for every grain
which isn't the same
but wonderfully unique
and beautifully made.
Thank you,
for creating the sand
that gets stuck
between my toes.

Father God,
Thank you
for sand,
soft and running
through our hand,
thick and squidgy,
when it's wet and squishy;
sand that we can
transform into a castle
surrounded by a moat
or a car or a boat,
sand that's sometimes
as hot as burning coals,
and sometimes as cold
as ice,
sand that says to the sea
'stop'
and sand that says to me
'come'
and have some
fun.

Pebbles

Heavenly Father,
Thank you
for pebbles,
so smooth and so round,
stones that are found
on the sand,
that we can hold
in our hand
and throw into the sea,
skim across the water
and watch them bounce,
see the ripples they make
as we drop them
and watch them
fall into the deep blue
sea.

The sea

Father God,
Thank you for the sea.
It's a lot, lot bigger
than me.
It's deep
and it's wide,
deeper than a hole in the
  ground,
wider than a house
and a building
and a plane
and a field
and a lake.
It's amazing to see
how huge,
how vast
the ocean is
compared to me.

Father God,
Thank you for the sea,
sparkling bright blue,
under a hot summer's sun.
Thank you
for the sound of the surf
as it rolls onto the shore,
a sound as old as time,
the steady rhythm of creation.
Thank you
for life under the sea
that lives and swims
deep down in the ocean's
  depths,
brilliant creatures
with fascinating features,
a rainbow of colours,
a rich mixture of textures,
all giving glory
to the artist of the ocean,
the creator of the sea
and all that we can see.

Waves

Heavenly Father,
Thank you
for the waves
that lap the sandy shore.
Thank you that the waves
never get tired
or find it a bore,
but keep on
rolling in
and in
and in.
Day in,
day out,
day in,
day out,
year in,
year out,
year in,
year out,
the waves
keep waving,
keep coming,
keep going,
and I love it!

Caring Creator

Father God,
Thank you
that every hair on my head
is numbered,
every grain of sand
is counted,
every sparrow that falls
is remembered,
every person on this planet
is counted
as being loved by you.

Creator God

Creator God,
Thank you
that you
are bigger than me,
bigger than all I can see,
bigger than the universe,
bigger than the galaxies,
bigger and bigger
than anything
because you
created
EVERYTHING.

The countryside

Father God,
Thank you
for the green, green, green
countryside.
It would be no good
for playing hide and seek
because there is so much of it,
and it's everywhere,
if we look.
Lots of countryside
in shades of green, green,
green,
all there
to be seen.

Rainbows

Creator God,
Thank you
for rainbows,
a multitude
of many colours,
a bright reminder
on a rainy day
that you keep your promises
every single day.

Flowers

Creator God,
Thank you
for daffodils,
tulips,
roses,
carnations
and all colourful
flowery creations
that smell so well
and look so swell.

The sun

Father God,
Thank you
for the sun
that feels warm on our face,
and shines brightly
from far-away space.
Thank you
that it's parked
in just the right place
to give us light
and help us see
that everything was created
the way it should be.

Light

Loving God,
Thank you
for light,
whether it's brilliant and bright
or murky and grey,
it's always with us,
every single day,
and means that we can see
this wonderful world
that you created.

Waterfalls

Life-giving God,
Thank you
for waterfalls
that splash
and crash
onto rocks
and stones,
that splash
and bash
over pebbles
and twigs,
that dash
and rush
over mountains
and hills.

Stars

Father God,
Thank you
for the stars
at night
that shine
so bright,
glow with
brilliant light,
a wonderful
glorious sight,
shining from a
great height,
shining millions
of light-years away
TONIGHT.

Rivers

Creator God,
Thank you
for rivers
that sparkle and shine
in the bright, summer sun.
Thank you
for rivers
that burble and murmur
and sing their own song.
Thank you
for rivers
that run on
and on and on.

Variety

Father God,
Thank you
that out of a world
of six billion people
not one of them
is the same
and each one of them
is known by name
by you;
thank you
that you care for us
and love each one of us
the same.

Beautiful world

Heavenly Father,
Thank you
for the world
we live in,
our big, beautiful blue
planet,
full of oceans,
tall mountains,
green fields
and so much stunning scenery.
Please help us
to look after our planet
and keep it clean,
please help us
to recycle our waste
and not to waste
this wonderful world
that you have created.

Bodies

Creator God,
Thank you
for our bodies.
Thank you for
long legs,
short arms,
red hair,
brown eyes,
big ears,
little noses,
white teeth,
freckled faces,
blue eyes,
blond hair,
short legs,
long arms,
small ears,
rosy cheeks,
pale skin,
brown skin,
red skin,
yellow skin,
black skin,
skinny legs,
scabby knees
from climbing trees!
We all have different bodies,
and no body
is the same . . .
. . . thanks to you!

Body parts

Father God,
Thank you
for our hands.
With our hands
we can make things,
write stories,
throw a ball,
catch,
shake hands,
stroke a dog,
paint a picture,
eat an apple,
make a snowman,
cook food in a pan,
decorate a Christmas tree,
hang up a stocking,
open presents,
play with our toys,
press the keys on our computer,
feel the coolness of a sparkling
river,
touch the furry caterpillar,
put them together
and say a prayer.

Father God,
Thank you
for our feet.
With our feet
we can kick a ball,
run on the grass,
stand up,
walk up

a mountain,
cross the road,
go and see our friends
who live on a different street,
dance to the rhythm and beat
of a song,
feel the sand between our toes,
splash in the sea,
run wild and free
on our two wonderful
feet.

Father God,
Thank you
for our eyes.
With our eyes
we can see the clear blue sky,
the vast ocean,
the smallest flea,
a bird in a tree,
a buzzing bee,
blades of grass blowing in the
breeze,
the colours of the rainbow,
a crimson sunset,
the winter frost on the icy
ground,
the rain running down the
window pane.
With our eyes
we can see
our family
and friends,
people who love us
and care for us.
We thank you
for our eyes
which help us to see
this wonderful world around
us.

Father God,
Thank you
for our ears.
With our ears
we can hear the birds singing,
the cat meowing,
dogs barking,
the hamster's wheel running,
rivers gurgling,
waves surfing,
aeroplanes flying,
cars revving,
children playing,
teachers teaching,
phones ringing,
and if we listen very, very
quietly
maybe
the sound of the earth
rotating.

Me

Life-giving God,
Thank you
that you made me
the way I am.
The colour of my eyes,
the shape of my face,
the length of my legs,
the colour of my skin,
every single thing
about me
is all down to you
thinking of me,
even before
I was born.
Father God,
that thought
AMAZES me!
And all I want to say
is a great, big
THANK YOU!

Life

Lord,
We thank you
for LIFE,
it is a gift,
a precious, precious
gift,
and each new day
is like a present,
waiting to be unwrapped,
waiting to be opened.
Lord,
we thank you
for this priceless gift
and pray
that by the way
we make the most of it,
we will show you
just how grateful we are.

Family and friends

Family

Our Father God,
Thank you
for our families,
the people we live with,
share a home with,
share our food with,
share our lives with,
have fun with,
fall out with, and
make up with.
Please help
my family
to see the good
in one another,
to be patient
with each other,
to remember
that families
are special
and come in all shapes
and sizes.

Home

Father God,
Thank you
for houses
for bungalows
for flats
for cottages
for igloos
for huts
for tents
for caravans
for farms
for ranches
for boats
for barges
for all the different places
that we can call
home.

Friendship

Loving God,
Thank you
for friends –
people who like us,
care about us,
play with us,
share with us,
stay with us.
When we're sad,
when we're bad,
when we're mad
and angry,
thank you
for friends
who love us
at all times.
Please help us
to be good friends
to others.

Friends

Father God,
Thank you for friends.
Friends are special,
friends are fun,
friends are great,
friends are neat.
Yet . . . sometimes
we fall out.
We break up our friendships
by unkind words,
by doing selfish things.
Please help us
to make up
with our friends,
to say sorry
and to forgive,
so we can be friends . . .
. . . again.

The joy of words

Lord,
Thank you
for the joy of talking,
sharing our secrets
with our friends,
laughing and joking
with our mates,
answering questions
in our class,
having conversations
about our favourite things,
deep discussions
on various topics,
shouting for our team
to win,
or whispering the words
'I love you'
to our family.
We thank you
for the words
we can say
to express
whatever we are feeling
every single day.

School life

New school year

Father God,
Thank you
for this brand-new school year.
We pray
that we will make the most of
it,
do our best,
try our hardest,
listen well,
do what we are told
and always remember to say
'please' and 'thank you.'
We pray
that you will bless our teachers.
Give them wisdom,
grant them patience,
give them strength,
grant them grace.
Thank you
for them,
for the wonderful work they
do,
for the special things
they teach us,
the special people that they are.
Please help all of us
to make you
the centre of our community
and listen to you,
the greatest teacher
of them all.

End of term

Thank you, Father God,
For this school year,
for all we've learned,
for all we've done,
for all the fun,
for all the smiles
from all of our friends.
Thank you
for this our school,
for all who've worked
so hard this year.
We pray you will bless them
and help them to rest and be
refreshed.

School trips

Lord,
Thank you
for school trips,
educational visits,
to libraries and museums,
entertaining visits
to the theatre and cinema,
exciting visits
to the countryside and seaside;
for all the places
that we go.
Please keep us safe
and help us to learn
as well as enjoy.

Lessons

Father God,
Thank you
for History,
where we can learn
about our ancestors,
wars, famines and earthquakes
and all kinds of disasters
from far-away countries,
foreign cultures,
kings and queens
from the past,
Ancient Rome and Egypt,
civilisations which didn't last.
Thank you
that there are so many lessons
we can learn from history.
Please help us
not to repeat the mistakes
of yesterday
but build a better future
and a bright tomorrow
by the way we live
today.

Father God,
Thank you
for Physical Education,
learning how to play
all kinds of games like
football,
netball,
hockey and cricket,
how to bowl a ball
and try to take a wicket,
how to kick a ball
and try to score a goal,
how to catch a ball
and not let it fall,
how to keep our bodies
nice and fit
with so many exercises
that we can jump to it!

Father God,
Thank you
for Maths,
please help us
to have a positive attitude
to learning,
and not to be negative
in our studying.
Thank you
that you want to add
good things to our lives
and take away all that is
negative and bad.
Thank you
that we can always
count on you
to help us.

Father God,
Thank you
for English,
for the wonder of words
and the power of words,
please help us
to use our speech wisely

and carefully
so our words
bless
and not curse.
Please help us
to comprehend
how much you love us
and to read
your story
and hear what you have to say
to us.

Father God,
Thank you
for I.T.
and for computers,
it's great to learn
how to use them
and see how clever they are,
and all the amazing things
that we can do on them.
Thank you
that each one of our minds
is more complex
and far cleverer
than the smartest computer.

Father God,
Thank you
for Geography,
where we can learn
about distant lands,
hot places with scorching
sands,
countries which are
mountainous,
and nations that are flat.
Thank you
that we can see
the wonder
and the beauty
of so many brilliant,
colourfully different places
in this big amazing world
that you have made.

Father God,
Thank you
for Science,
learning to understand
some of the wonders
in the world
around us,
doing experiments,
watching and seeing
how things work
and why things work.
Thank you
that you had the ability to
create
and to make our world
and everything within it,
including us.

Father God,
Thank you
for R.E.,
for learning about faith,
stories that are

thousands of years old
and yet as up to date
as our daily papers.
Thank you
for the lessons of life
that we can learn
from these timeless tales
which teach us
how to treat one another
and respect each other,
how to love one another
and help each other;
thank you
for faith.

Father God,
Thank you
for Art,
for the opportunity
of creating,
of making,
of decorating,
of designing,
of painting,
of drawing,
of colouring,
all kinds of shapes,
all sorts of patterns,
all types of pictures;
thank you
for giving us
the abilities
for artistic creativities.

Playground prayer

In our playground
there is lots of noise
from all the boys
and all the girls.
There are shouts and screams,
groans and moans,
cries and sighs,
laughter and fun.
We thank you
for our times of play
and pray
that we will be safe today
happy
in our play.

Playtimes

Lord,
Thank you
for our break times
and lunch times,
and for all the times
that we can go out and play.
Thank you
for the games that we can play,
and the fun we can have
with our friends.
Please help us
to not just think about
what we want to play
but about what others
want to do today.

Please help us
not to exclude
but to include
people,
so that not just some,
but everyone,
can have fun.

Wet playtimes

Lord,
On a day
when the clouds are grey
and gloomy
and the rain is pouring
like a non-stop
leaking tap
and we can't play outside,
please help us
to make the most
of our nice warm school,
to enjoy playing indoor games,
reading books,
swapping stories
and jokes
with our friends.
Please help us
to make the most
of our wet day plays
we pray.

Visitors

Lord,
Thank you
for all the people
who visit our school,
ministers,
nurses,
police,
guest speakers,
parents
and all kinds of helpers
who care about us
and come to teach us
so many different things;
please help us
to show respect
to those who so generously
give their time
to help us.

People at school

Father God,
Thank you
for our time at school,
for our teachers
for our dinnerladies
for our cleaners
for our school secretaries
for our caretakers
for our friends
who all make us
happy and glad
that we can all come back
tomorrow.

Morning and evening prayers

Morning prayers

Father God,
Thank you
for this new day.
Please help us
to make the most of it
in work, rest and play.

Father God,
Thank you
that whatever I'm feeling –
sad or bad,
good or glad,
lonely or mad –
you are always the same.
You are always loving,
always good,
always kind,
always fair,
always there.
Thank you
that you know all about me.
You know how I am feeling,
you know how I am doing
and you care for me,
this new day.

Creator God,
Thank you
for the light of another new
day.
Even if the sun doesn't shine
and the rain sets in,
we can still enjoy this freshly
created day.
Thank you.

Evening prayer

Loving Heavenly Father,
Thank you
for the day that we've had,
whether some of it was good
or some of it was bad.
We thank you
for being there,
always there
even when we sleep,
even when we dream
you are wide awake.
Thank you that you will be
there to greet us
tomorrow.

Seasonal prayers

Spring

Father God,
Thank you
for the springtime,
for the first sight
of new life.
Buds beginning to open,
flowers starting to wake up
out of the sleepy earth.
Thank you
for the colours,
for the flowers . . .

. . . those sun-coloured
daffodils
swaying gently
in the breeze.
Thank you
for the lambs
racing through the grass,
bleating and
baaing
now that spring has been
sprung.

Summer

Father God,
Thank you for summer days,
never-ending light,
sunny outdoor plays.
Thank you
for sun and sea,
big blue sky and
sandcastles for me.
Thank you
for the summer holidays
that stretch
as far as the horizon,
and seem to last forever.

Autumn

Lord God,
Thank you
for the burning,
fiery leaves,
the golden colours
as the season mellows
and autumn changes
the window dressing
of the trees.

Winter

Father God,
Thank you for snow and ice,
white frosted paths
and the frozen duckponds.
Thank you
for the crimson sky,
the early golden sunsets,
for seeing our breath
hanging in the air,
telling us that winter is here.

Christmas prayers

Jesus
Father God,
Thank you
for this time of Advent,
this time of preparing,
this time of thinking
what Christmas is all about.
Why you sent your Son,
why the wise men wandered,
why the star shone brightly,
why the angels sang
  beautifully,
why the shepherds ran
  delightedly,
why the world was waiting
  expectantly.

For a Saviour
Father God,
At this time of year
when we think about
what we want,
please help us
to think about
what we can give.

The season
Father God,
Thank you
for this special season,
please help us
to remember the reason:
your Son,
our Saviour
Jesus Christ.

Peace
Heavenly Father,
At this time of year
we pray for peace
to remove our fear.
Peace in our hearts
peace in our minds
peace in our lives
peace in our homes
peace in our school
peace in our land
peace in our world.
May we find
true peace
real lasting peace
with you.

The greatest gift
Father God,
Thank you
for Christmas
for snow and ice
for parties and presents
for cards and tinsel
for holidays and good food
for so many things.
We want to say
THANK YOU,
but most of all
we want to thank you
for the greatest gift
you gave the world – Jesus.

Gifts
Our Father God,
Thank you
for gifts,
for presents,
for things we don't have to buy.
Thank you
for grace,
your loving kindness,
a gift from you,
that we can never afford,
but we can receive.

Eastertime

What's with the pancakes?
Father God,
Thank you
for pancakes
with sugar and syrup
or chocolate and lemon
or any kind of combination.
Please help us
to remember the reason
why we have pancake day,
a start of a new season,
the beginning of Lent,
a feast before the famish,
a time when people make sacrifices,
a time when we remember Jesus,
and what he sacrificed for us.

Forgiveness
Father God,
Thank you
for Jesus
your Son
who died a death
so horrible
so painful
so brutal
that we might be
forgiven.

Creator God,
Thank you for Easter.
At this time of year
we think about new life,
we see it in the fields
with the tiny newborn lambs,
we see it in the trees
with the sprouting of tiny
new buds,
we see it on the earth
with the daffodils springing
out of their beds.
We see new life everywhere
and remember an empty tomb,
frightened, startled disciples,
confused, bewildered soldiers
all struggling to understand
the new life that had begun
in Jesus.

Harvest

Dear Father God,
Thank you
for the farmer,
for the fields and the crops
which the combined harvester
goes out and chops.
Thank you
for the food
the riches on our plate,
delicious tastes, pleasing smells
which we think are great.
Thank you
for the harvest,
the food that helps us live,
please help us to share it and
teach us how to give.

Remembrance day

Our Father God,
Thank you
for all of the soldiers
who fought for our freedom,
who stood up
for what is right.
Please help us
to stand up today,
be brave and strong
in always doing
the right thing.

Father God,
Thank you
for your Son,
Jesus,
who gave his life,
so that we may have
freedom
in our lives
today.

Dear Father God,
Thank you
for all the people
who were willing
and prepared
to sacrifice
and give their lives
so that we may live
freely
today.

Firework night

Loving God,
Thank you
for fireworks,
for the ones that EXPLODE
with a loud BANG,
for fireworks
that fizzle and crackle,
for fireworks
that whizz,
for fireworks
that burst into beautiful
colours,
for fireworks
that spin in a cartwheel,
for fireworks
that make and create
the Niagara Falls,
for fireworks
of all colours, shapes and sizes
we thank you.

Father God,
Thank you
for bonfire night,
for fire and smoke,
for toffee apples and hot dogs,
for sparklers and more
sparklers,
for fireworks and even more
fireworks,
we thank you for this
wonderful night
and pray that you would help
us to be safe tonight.

Thinking of others

Thinking of others

Loving Heavenly Father,
Thank you
for my family
for my home
for my food
for my friends
for my school.
Please help me
to remember
the children
who have no family
no home
no food
no friends
no school.

It's so very hard
to imagine
what it must be like
to have so little
or nothing at all.
Please help
the children today.
Please show us
what we can do
to show your love.
Please show us
how we can be
your hands and your feet
giving help
showing kindness
showing that we care.

Everyone matters

Dear Father God,
Sometimes I act as if the world revolves
around me,
but there are lots and lots of people
I don't even see
in this big wide world.
Please help me to see
that everyone is just as important
as me.

Other people

Father God,
Thank you
that you made this world
full of lots of different people.
Some of them look like me
some of them don't,
some of them talk like me
some of them don't,
some of them live near me
some of them don't,
but all of them,
every single one of them
is special to you.

Giving

Loving Heavenly Father,
Thank you
that giving a little
can make a lot of difference;
one kind word,
a small act of kindness
all act like a pebble
thrown into the sea,
as we watch
and we see
ripples
spreading out,
reaching out
to others,
in other parts
of the world,
where our help,
our small gift
can make a big, big
world of difference.

Poverty

Father God,
Please help us
to make poverty
history,
a thing of the past,
something that will not last
another lifetime.
Please help us
to be a lifeline
to those who are drowning
in a sea of poverty,
overwhelmed
by wave upon wave
of calamity,
causing poverty so bad
it's like a tidal wave,
all consuming,
a debt
that is never ending,
please help us
to put an end
to this worldwide
problem.

Children in Need

Father God,
Thank you
for 'Children In Need'
and the chance
to do what we can
and give what we're able.
Thank you
that you are able
to take small offerings
like a few fish
and some loaves of bread
and feed multitudes.
Please help our small offerings
make a world of difference.

Father God,
Thank you
that every child
is precious
in your sight
and every need
is known
by you.
Please help us
to see the need
and do all we can
to help.

Father God,
Thank you
for charity,
the opportunities
provided
to think of others
and to give to others.
Please help us
to be charitable
constantly
and not just
once or twice a year,
but every day
in some small way
to give
something,
do
anything
we can
to help,
be kind,
be generous,
to others.

Father God,
In some way or another
we all need
charity:
people being generous
to us,
giving us their time,
the gift of a smile,
passing on a kind word,
helping us with a problem.
In some small way
help us
to brighten up someone's day
today.

Father God,
Thank you
for events
that help raise
the profile
of charities,
that help raise
awareness
of issues
that we need
to deal with.
Please help us
to have wisdom
in how to be as effective
as we can
in helping,
in understanding,
in caring
for others.

General prayers

The nature and character of God

Dear Father God,
Thank you
that you are Alpha,
the beginning,
and you are Omega,
the end,
you are like a circle,
we cannot see
where you begin
or where you end,
but we know
that you are there
and have been here
forever.

Father God,
Thank you
that wherever we are
and whatever we've done,
you are there
and you care.
Thank you
that we can talk to you
in prayer.

Response prayers

Praise

Father God,
In all the good times
  we praise you,
in all the hard times
  we praise you,
in all our schooldays
  we praise you,
in all our holidays
  we praise you,
in all our lives
  we praise you.

Thanks

Creator God,
For our families
  we thank you,
for our friends
  we thank you,
for our school
  we thank you,
for our world
  we thank you.

Mercy

When we have said bad things
have mercy on us.
When we have done wrong
  things
have mercy on us.

When we have been rude
have mercy on us.
When we have been greedy
have mercy on us.
When we have been selfish
have mercy on us.
And please help us
to forgive others
as you
have forgiven us.

Jobs

Father God,
Thank you for the letters that
the postman brings.
The rattling of the milk
bottles as the dawn chorus
sings.
The pilot who flies the planes
with big, big wings.
The food in the shops that the
lorry brings.
The emergency rescuers as
the siren rings.
We thank you
for all the
different jobs,
for all the
different people
and for all the differences
they make to our lives.

Transport

Lord,
Thank you
for cars, planes and trains,
for bicycles, buses and balloons.
Thank you
for so many different ways
in which we can travel today.
Thank you
for the people
who invented them.
Thank you
for the people
who drive the vehicles.
Thank you
for the journeys
that we can go on.

For those in authority

Loving God,
Thank you
for our government,
thank you
for people willing to take big
responsibilities.
Please help them
to listen well
and decide wisely
for everyone in our country.

Father God,
Thank you
for the royal family,
thank you
for all the things they do
for our country.
Please protect them,
please bless them
and please grant them
wisdom.

Words

Loving Heavenly Father,
Thank you
for words.
With words we can talk
and say what we think,
what we feel,
what we like,
what we don't like.
We can share our secrets
with our friends,
we can share our dreams
and our hopes.
We can share our thoughts,
tell our jokes,
we can say all kinds of things.
Please help us
to be kind
in what we say.
Please help us
to think
about what we are saying
and how others may be
feeling.
Please help us
to help others
with our words
today.

Food

Father God,
Thank you
for food,
for pizzas
and all the different toppings,
for all the food we buy
when we go shopping.
For burgers,
for fish,
for lots of tasty things
we can have in our dish.
For 'cracking cheese'
that would please
Wallace and Gromit.
We thank you
for all the wonderful food
that we can eat
and pray
that we will share
the plenty we have
with those
who have so little.

Ice-creams

Loving God,
Thank you
for ice-creams
on a hot sunny day,
delicious flavours like
chocolate,
raspberry,
cherry,
vanilla,
mint,
strawberry,
chocolate chip.
So many wonderful flavours
that we can savour
and taste
on a summer holiday
lounging on a beach.

Talents and abilities

Creator God,
Thank you
for the talents
that you have given us,
for the abilities
that we have.
Please help us
to use them
and develop them
as we should.

Walks

Lord,
Thank you
for walks
that we can go on,
short walks,
long walks,
medium-sized walks,
walks to the shops,
walks to school,
walks in the country,
walks in town,
walks in winter,
walks in summer,
spring and autumn too,
walks up hills,
walks down dales,
walks along city streets,
walks by riverbanks,
walks on sandy beaches,
walks on rocky ledges,
we thank you
for the joy of walking.

God is with me

Lord,
Some days
I feel like singing,
some days
I feel like crying;
some days
I feel like dancing,
some days
I feel like curling up
into a ball
and hiding away;
some days
I want to play
forever,
some days
I want everything
to go away
forever;
some days
are great,
some days
I just hate.
But I thank you
that on each and every day
you promise
to be with me
and help me
because
you love me.

Trusting God

Father God,
in a world
full of broken promises
we can
trust you.

In a world
with big problems
we can trust in you.

Lord,
When trouble comes
we often want to run
to the hills,
head for cover,
hide away
and hope that the troubles
will go away,
but often they don't
and won't
if we do nothing
about them.

Lord,
When troubles come
please help us
to look to the hills
and to the one
who made them,
the one who never sleeps
nor slumbers
but watches
over
us.

Hope

Loving Heavenly Father,
We thank you
for hope
when all seems hopeless,
we thank you
that you find us
when we feel lost,
we thank you
for love
when we feel lonely,
we thank you
for light
when we are in the dark,
we thank you
for peace
when we have troubled minds,
we thank you
for your gentleness
when we feel fragile,
we thank you
for your kindness and goodness
when life is harsh and horrible,
we thank you,
for being faithful
when we have been let down.
We thank you,
Father God,
we thank you
for being
you.

Trust

Father God,
We thank you,
that you know
everything.
Sometimes
things happen
that we don't understand,
things happen
that we don't like,
and we wonder why.
And we don't know why.
Please help us
in our times of being in the dark
to know that you,
the true light of the world,
are with us
and can help us.
Please help us
to see your light
in a dark, dark situation
and in a dark, dark world.
Please help us
to let your light
SHINE.

Death

Lord Jesus,
You know what it's like
to lose a friend.
You know what it's like
to see your friends crying
because someone they love
has died.
Lord Jesus,
you wept
when Lazarus, your friend,
died.
You wept
when you saw his sisters,
and you shed your tears
for someone you loved,
even though you brought
Lazarus
back to life.
Lord Jesus,
thank you
that you understand how we
feel
and even though we believe
in life after death,
we know it's OK
to cry
because
you wept.

Father God,
Thank you,
that you are a God
who comforts,
like the warmth of the
summer sun,
like the voice of our favourite
friend,
like the person and the place
we love the most,
you comfort us and are all of
these things
and much, much more.
You bring us comfort
when we are upset,
you care for us
when we cry,
and you carry our burdens
when we can't carry them any
more,
and you carry us
when we can't go on any more.
Thank you.

Heavenly Father,
When the ones
we love
have gone,
passed on,
it can feel like they've left
a great big hole
in our lives
that no one can ever fill
and we don't know how
we're going to cope.
Thank you,
that because of you
we do have hope,
hope for our loved ones,
that we will see them again,
one day,
in heaven;
hope for our lives,
as our journey goes on,
and the thoughts
and special memories
of the ones we love
we will take with us
and carry them safely in our hearts
for ever.

Father God,
We pray
for those today
who are sad and upset,
who are grieving
for the ones they love.
We want to wrap
our thoughts and prayers
around them,
comfort and protect them.
Father God,
please help them to know
how much we care,
how much we feel for their loss,
for their heartache and pain,
and as we pray
our hearts
go out to them.

Prayers based on Scripture

Prayers from the Psalms (The Message)

In trouble

Psalm 40

I waited and waited and
waited for God.
At last he looked; finally he
listened.
He lifted me out of the ditch,
pulled me from deep mud.
He stood me up on a solid
rock
to make sure I wouldn't slip.
He taught me how to sing the
latest God-song,
a praise-song to our God.

In gratitude

Psalm 34

I bless God every chance I get;
my lungs expand with his
praise.
I live and breathe God;
if things aren't going well,
hear this and be happy:
join me in spreading the news;
together let's get the word out.
God met me more than
halfway,
he freed me from my anxious
fears.

In forgiveness

Psalm 32

Count yourself lucky, how
happy you must be –
you get a fresh start,
your slate's wiped clean.
Count yourself lucky –
God holds nothing against you
and you're holding nothing
back from him.

In praise and worship

Psalm 33

Good people, cheer God!
Right-living people sound
best when praising.
Use guitars to reinforce your
Hallelujahs!
Play his praise on a grand
piano!
Invent your own new song to
him;
give him a trumpet fanfare.

In trust

Psalm 16

Keep me safe, O God,
I've run for dear life to you.
I say to God, 'Be my Lord!'
Without you, nothing makes
sense.

Prayers from the Psalms (NIV)

In security

In you, O Lord, I have taken refuge.
Psalm 31:1

You God
and you alone
are the shelter from the storm,
the one who can keep me
from all harm
because by your right arm
you can save me.
Like a blanket,
you wrap your love
around me,
you hide me
in your wings
and my spirit just sings
and sings your praise,
all of my days,
I want to thank and praise,
raise my voice and say
you are my rock,
the rock that can't be rocked,
the rock that can't be rolled
and I will put my security,
all of my certainty
in you.

In caring

Blessed is he who has regard for the weak.
Psalm 41:1

If I have plenty,
help me to give to those without.
If I am strong,
help me to help those who are weak.
If I am good at maths,
help me to be a friend people can count on.
If I am good at English,
help me to be a friend people can talk to.
If I have gifts and talents,
help me to use them and bless others.
If I have a heart,
please help me to care.

In direction

Your word is a lamp to my feet and a light for my path.
Psalm 119:105

Your word is a guide,
a light from which I won't hide.
Your word is full of instruction,
giving me a clear direction.

Your word is for today,
as well as yesterday.
Your word is full of goodness,
real, wonderful wholeness.
Your word is beautiful and
true,
drawing me near to you.

In need

As the deer pants for streams of water, so my soul pants for you, O God.
Psalm 42:1

I'm thirsty,
but not for Coca-cola,
or lemonade,
or orange juice,
or appletiser.
I'm thirsty,
but not for
blackcurrant,
Ribena,
grapefruit juice
or any other tantalising drink.
I'm thirsty for you God,
thirsty deep inside,
thirsty to know you God.
I want to drink in
all that is good,
all that is right,
all that is healthy
and I'm not talking about
something liquid
but a right way of living.

In speech

My heart is stirred by a noble theme as I recite my verses for the king; my tongue is the pen of a skilful writer.
Psalm 45:1

O God,
your story is good,
very good,
excellent,
the best story there is,
it can run rings around
The Lord of the Rings!
Your story is about everyone
and anyone can read it
and know how you saved
a nation.
Know how you saved
a person.
Saved people from
a den of lions,
from the belly of a big fish,
from a giant of a man.
O God,
you can save,
and I want to savour who you
are,
a Saviour God,
and I want to speak
and I want to tell
of your great
and glorious
salvation.

In stillness

Be still and know that I am God.
Psalm 46:10

I'm often in a rush,
running so fast,
as if I'm going to run
right in to tomorrow.
I'm always busy doing things,
playing out,
playing in,
playing on
my computer.
I'm always up to something,
even when I shouldn't be.
I need to stop sometimes
and be still,
calm down,
sit down
and settle down.
Be still
not just in my body
but in my mind
and my heart
and know that no matter what
is going on
and no matter what
is happening
and I am doing
you are still God,
always have been,
always are
and always will be.

Prayers based on Psalm 119

Your word is a lamp to my feet and a light for my path.
Psalm 119:105

Father God,
Thank you
that your word
is like a light
being switched on
on a dark, dark morning;
your word
helps us to see
what is right and
helps us to know
which way to go.
Your word
is like a lamp
leading us,
guiding us,
so that we can see
where we're going
and know that what we are doing
is right.
Please help us
to keep looking
to your word
so that we will live our lives
in the light
of your ways.

Turn my heart towards your statutes and not towards selfish gain.
Psalm 119:36

Dear Father God,
Please help us
to live our lives
not thinking about
how much we can gain
but how much we can give,
not thinking about how much
we have
but how much we love,
not how much we think
we are the best,
but how we can do
our best for others,
not how much we can
serve ourselves
but how much we can
serve others,
please help us
to be like Jesus.

May your unfailing love come to me, O Lord, your salvation according to your promise.
Psalm 119:41

Father God,
in this life
lots of things fail us,
our cars won't start,
the TV is on the blink,
there's gunge in the sink,
our friends fall out,
the rain keeps us inside,
we can't find that THING!
And people we love
get ill.
Sometimes life can be sad
and life can be hard,
but in all things
and at all times
your love never
ever
fails us;
you never break down,
you never go on the blink,
you never fall ill,
you never leave us,
you are always there
and you always,
always care
for us.

All your words are true; and your righteous laws are eternal.
Psalm 119:160

Heavenly Father,
Thank you
that all your words are true,
all of them are honest,
you never tell a lie,
not even a small one,
or what we might call
'a white one',
you never bend the truth

or try to deceive,
but always speak with honesty
and it's wonderful to know
that we can trust
in your truth.
Please help us
to be honest
with you and
with one another too.

May my lips overflow with praise, for you teach me your decrees.
Psalm 119:171

Father God,
Thank you
that there is so much
to thank you for,
for your goodness,
your kindness,
your graciousness
to us,
for your love,
for your peace,
for your forgiveness,
that you've granted us,
for your Son,
for Jesus,
who died for us,
for your Spirit,
your desire
to help us
and live with us.
We thank you
and praise you
for who you are,
how great you are
and how great
is the love that you
have lavished on us,
that we can be called
children of God.

Prayers on the fruit of the Spirit

But the fruit of the Spirit is love, joy, peace, patience, kindness, goodness, faithfulness, gentleness and self-control.
Galatians 5:22

Lord,
Thank you
for all the times
when people have been patient
with me.
Thank you
for the times
when people have waited
and not rushed away.
Thank you
for the times
when my teachers
have explained things to me
again and again

and have patiently
waited
for me to understand.
Thank you
for your patience
with me
time and time again.
Please help me
to show patience
and be patient
with others.

Creator God,
Thank you
for the rainbow,
that it reminds
us
that you always,
always, always, always,
keep your promises.
Please help us
to keep our promises
too.

Loving Heavenly Father,
Before the world was made
you loved us.
Before we were born
you loved us.
When we do wrong things
you love us.
When Jesus died on the cross
he showed
you love us.

Loving Heavenly Father,
Thank you
for all the many, many, many
things
that bring us
happiness and joy.
Our family
our friends
our pets,
playing sport
playing music
playing games,
singing
acting
reading
writing
sunsets
sunrises
snow
snowmen
Christmas
presents
birthdays
parties.
Father God,
the list could go on and on.
There are so many things that
bring joy
and I want to thank you for
the joy
that you give
by loving us every single day.

Dear Father God,
Thank you
for kindness,
kind words
kind actions
kind thoughts
which help people
feel better,
that make the world
a better place.
Please help us
to be kind
in all that we say
and do
today.

Life-giving God,
Thank you
for peace,
the peace and quiet of the
countryside,
the peace that comes when all
is still and calm
and thank you
for the peace that you promise
when things are far from well,
the promise to be with us
and help us.

Dear Lord,
Thank you
that there are times to play,
times to eat
and times to work.
Sometimes I want to eat
biscuits
before tea,
or play
before I've finished my work.
Please help me to wait
and be self-controlled.

Lord,
Thank you
that you are good,
you are never bad,
never naughty,
never unkind,
but always, constantly,
consistently good.
All that you do is good.
All that you say is good.
Please help us
to be like you.

Father God,
Thank you
for your love,
your faithful love.
As reliable as sunrise,
as dependable as sunset,
deeper than the oceans,
higher than the mountains,
bigger than the universe,
gentler than a summer breeze,
warmer than the sun and
brighter than the moon.

Thank you
for choosing to love
us.
Please help us
to choose
to love
today.

Loving Heavenly Father,
Sometimes
when I pick something up at
home
Mum shouts out:
'BE CAREFUL, THAT'S
REALLY FRAGILE. DON'T
BREAK IT!'
Some things do break easily,
especially if you drop them.
People are fragile too.
If we say horrid things,
it hurts their feelings.
If we hit them,
it bruises their skin.
Please help us today
to be gentle
with one another
in all that we do
and say.

Worry and anxiety

Come to me, all you who are weary and burdened, and I will give you rest.
Matthew 11:28

Loving Father,
You know how my mind
works
and how sometimes
it works in overdrive,
how I worry
about all sorts of things,
about almost everything;
I worry about
so much stuff
I feel like my mind's
going to blow
with all the overload.
Please help me to offload
all my cares,
all my concerns
onto you,
because you
care for me
and are concerned about
every part
of my life;
thank you.

Do not be anxious about anything, but in everything, by prayer and petition, with thanksgiving, present your requests to God.
Philippians 4:6

Father God,
Thank you
that I can give you
whatever is bothering me,
whatever is worrying me,
whatever is troubling me;
thank you
that it is no trouble to you
and you can help me through;
thank you.

Therefore I tell you, do not worry about your life, what you will eat or drink; or about your body, what you will wear. Is not life more important than food, and the body more important than clothes?
Matthew 6:25

Creator God,
Thank you
for food
and drink
and all the other things in life
that I think
are important:
like the clothes I wear,
the way I comb my hair,
the body
that you've given me,
and all the things
I can do and play
every single day.

Please help me
not to worry
about all of these
important things
but to know
that the thing
I really must do
is to trust in you.

Look at the birds of the air; they do not sow or reap or stow away in barns, and yet your heavenly Father feeds them. Are you not much more valuable than they?
Matthew 6:26

Life-giving God,
Thank you
for the birds of the air
that can fly anywhere
and seem to have nothing
to worry
or care about,
not when you
feed them
and give them
enough to eat.

They don't have to go out to work
or buy meals from the shops
or put bread in their baskets
at the supermarkets.
Thank you
that you have provided food
for the animal world.
Please help us
to make sure
that we don't take away
the food
that they need
because of our greed;
please help us
to think about
the animals
that you have created
and the ways in which
you have made the world
their meal table.

Who of you by worrying can add a single hour to his life?
Matthew 6:27

Father God,
Please help me
to know
that worry can never add anything
but it can take away.
It can take away my peace,
leave me in pieces,
make me feel nervous,
fearful and tearful.
It can take away
my fun,
my happiness,
my love of life.

Please help me
to know
that the hours I waste
worrying
can never be replaced.

Please help
replace
my worries
with the knowledge
that you are there
and that you care
for me.

Prayers based on The Lord's Prayer

Our Father

Father God,
Thank you
that we can call you
Father
Our Father
Dad
Daddy

because that's who you are,
the Father of humankind,
the Maker of us all
and we thank you
that we can call
on you,
depend on you
anytime,
night
and day
as we pray
'Our Father'.

Who is in heaven

Dear Father,
Thank you
for heaven,
a place that is perfect,
somewhere that is called
Paradise.
It's hard to imagine
a place that we haven't seen
not even in holiday brochures,
a place that we haven't been to
but we know
it is going to be beyond good
because
you are there.

Hallowed be your name

Heavenly Father,
Your name is special,
holy,
separate,
different from any others;
because no one
in the whole of creation
is the creator
but you,
no one can compare
with you,
no one;
and no one can be called God
but you.
Please help us
to use your name
and to say your name
with respect
and remember who it is
we are speaking to.

Your kingdom come

Father God,
Thank you
for your kingdom,
a kingdom
that has no geographical
boundaries,
a kingdom that starts
in our hearts:
the place
where your love and rule
start,

affecting the way we act,
the way we think,
and the ways in which we live.
In a world
where we see so many bad things
going on
in earthly kingdoms
we do pray for,
and long for,
your peace,
your love
and your kingdom
to come.

Your will be done on earth as it is in heaven

Loving God,
Thank you
that everything you do is good,
and all that you are is good,
every desire that you have is good,
and your will for us is good.
Please help us,
to say 'yes'
to you
and to say 'yes'
to your will
in our lives,
that we will do the things
and act in the ways
that will please you
by doing all that is right
and all that is good
and pleasing in your sight.

Give us this day our daily bread

Father God,
Thank you
for providing us
with all that we need
because you know
our needs
even before we ask.
Please help us
not to be full of greed
but to give to those
who are in need.

Forgive us our trespasses as we forgive those who trespass against us

Father God,
Thank you
that you do forgive us
when we say sorry
to you.
You wipe out what we've done wrong
like pressing delete
on a computer,
whatever we've done
vanishes from your screen
because you mean it
when you say
you will forgive us
when we confess to you.

Please help us
to be like you
and show grace
and forgiveness
to those
who are willing to say
'sorry'
to us.

Lead us not into temptation but deliver us from evil

Dear Lord,
You know all about us,
and the words that we say
and the things that we do.
You know
what tempts us
to be naughty.
Please help us
to be led by you
on the right path,
and not to go
in the wrong direction.
Please help us
pay attention
to you,
so that we will follow
where you lead us.
Thank you
that you can,
and you do,
protect us
from evil,
and lead us
in your ways
which are good.

Jesus is the 'I Am'

I am the good shepherd

Lord Jesus,
Thank you
that you are good,
good in every way
and good towards us;
every single day
you watch over us
and watch out for us
like a shepherd
watching his flock.
You look and you watch,
watch over us
and watch out for us
in a good, good way,
leading us always
in the right ways.

I am the bread of life

Lord Jesus,
Thank you
that you are the bread
of life,
the bread that we need,
the bread that will feed
our soul,
make us complete
and whole.

Our daily bread,
not the sliced loaf
that we eat,
but the life-giving Spirit
we can receive
and the love we can know
which helps us grow
more like you
every single day.

I am the gate

Lord Jesus,
Thank you
that you show us the way
to live our lives,
thank you
that you are the way
for us to live our lives
and we thank you
that you open the door
for us to go through,
and to follow you
in your glorious kingdom
of heaven.

I am the vine

Lord Jesus,
Thank you
for fruit,
for delicious apples, pears
and bananas, oranges
and mangos.
So many kinds of tasty,
  healthy fruit
that we can eat,
fruit that grows from fruit trees.
We thank you
for the fruit of your Spirit,
for love, joy, peace, patience,
  kindness, goodness,
  faithfulness,
  gentleness and self-control.
Please help us
to grow in our relationship
with you,
so we can grow more
of your wonderful, healthy
life-enhancing fruit.

I am the resurrection

Lord Jesus,
Thank you
that you are
the defeater of death,
and have shown us
that breathing our last breath
is not the end of the road.
Our journey over,
it is not a full stop
but a comma,
a pause
for new breath
after death,
a promise of a new chapter
beginning
with you for eternity
where life
is never ending.

Index of Subjects